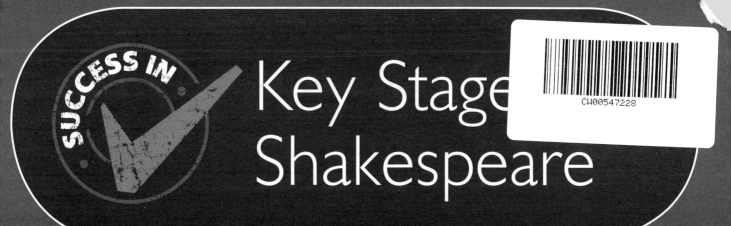

Success in Key Stage Shakespeare

MACBETH

MICHAEL JONES
and **KEVIN DYKE**

www.heinemann.co.uk
✓ Free online support
✓ Useful weblinks
✓ 24 hour online ordering

01865 888058

Inspiring generations

Introduction

Success in Key Stage 3 Shakespeare: **Macbeth** can help you improve the performance of all your students in the Key Stage 3 Shakespeare test. Together the **Success in Key Stage 3 Shakespeare: Macbeth** Student's Revision Book and Teacher's Notes provide a revision schedule of 15 lessons, ensuring that students engage with and revise character, theme, language and performance in the context of the set extracts. Once you have worked through the activities with your students, they will have explored the set scenes according to the four key areas of test questioning and supported these points with quotations from the set extracts.

The Teacher's Notes are available at www.heinemann.co.uk/literature. They include:
- a scheme of work for 15 revision lessons
- 15 lesson plans showing how the summary activities can be used to engage students and enhance understanding
- answers to all the activities in the Student's Revision Book.

By using **Success in Key Stage 3 Shakespeare: Macbeth** to revise for the Key Stage 3 tests, you can be secure in the knowledge that your students have been well prepared for the test and should feel confident and prepared to answer any question they may be asked.

Heinemann Educational Publishers
Halley Court, Jordan Hill, Oxford OX2 8EJ
Part of Harcourt Education

Heinemann is a registered trademark of
Harcourt Education Limited

© Harcourt Education, 2005

First published 2005

10 09 08 07 06
10 9 8 7 6 5 4 3

British Library Cataloguing in Publication Data is available
from the British Library on request.

10-digit ISBN: 0 43599808 0
13-digit ISBN: 978 0 435998 080

Designed by GD Associates
Typeset by ⁊ Tek-Art, Croydon, Surrey, UK
Printed in the UK by Thomson Litho Ltd
Illustrated by Andy Morris

Original illustrations © Harcourt Education Limited, 2005
Cover photo: © Alamy

Success in Key Stage 3 Shakespeare: *Macbeth*

Contents

The story of *Macbeth*

1 Witches meet Macbeth and Banquo on heath and hail them as future kings.

2 Macbeth and Banquo hear of Cawdor's treachery.

3 Duncan (the king) ennobles Macbeth but announces Malcolm as his heir. This means that Macbeth must kill his way to kingship.

4 Lady Macbeth learns that Duncan is coming to Glamis Castle. She knows that Macbeth will want the crown, but may not be able to betray and kill his king.

5 Lady Macbeth shames Macbeth into murdering his king.

6 Macbeth's unease about killing Duncan is evident – he sees a 'dagger of the mind' and fears eternal damnation.

7 After the murder Macbeth is in such a desperate state that Lady Macbeth has to return the daggers to the scene of the murder to make the dead grooms appear guilty.

8 Banquo's discovery of the dead Duncan and grooms makes the lords suspicious and prompts Malcolm and Donalbain to flee the country.

9 Banquo is murdered on Macbeth's orders, but his son Fleance escapes.

10 Lady Macbeth and Macbeth are at the banquet when Banquo's ghost appears, but only Macbeth can see it. The guests are amazed.

11 Macbeth seeks out the witches and hears their predictions, which deceive and dismay him.

12 King Macbeth orders the murder of Lady Macduff and her child.

13 Lady Macbeth, no longer Macbeth's true partner, is maddened by guilt.

14 Malcolm and the English army approach, and disguise themselves with boughs from Birnam Wood.

15 Macbeth is arming when he hears of the death of Lady Macbeth, and of Birnam Wood on the move. He begins to suspect that the weird sisters have tricked him.

16 Macduff kills Macbeth after revealing that he is not 'of woman born'. Malcolm becomes king of Scotland, with the witches watching and Fleance waiting.

Set extracts

Extract 1: Act 2, Scene 1 and Act 2, Scene 2

ACT 2, SCENE 1

A courtyard in the castle
Enter BANQUO, and FLEANCE bearing a <u>torch</u> before him

BANQUO
How goes the night, boy?

FLEANCE
The moon is down; I have not heard the clock.

BANQUO
And she goes down at twelve.

FLEANCE
I take't, 'tis later, sir.

BANQUO
Hold, take my sword. <u>There's husbandry in heaven,</u>
<u>Their candles are all out</u>. Take thee that too.
A <u>heavy</u> summons lies like <u>lead</u> upon me,
And yet I would not <u>sleep</u>. Merciful powers,
Restrain in me the <u>cursed thoughts</u> that nature
Gives way to in repose. Give me my sword.

Enter MACBETH, and a SERVANT with a torch

Who's there?

MACBETH
A <u>friend</u>.

BANQUO
What, sir, not yet at rest? The king's a-bed.
He hath been in unusual <u>pleasure</u>, and
Sent forth great <u>largess</u> to your offices.
This <u>diamond</u> he greets your wife withal,
By the name of <u>most kind</u> hostess, and shut up
In measureless content.

MACBETH
Being unprepared,
Our will became the servant to defect,
Which else should free have wrought.

BANQUO
All's well,
<u>I dreamt last night</u> of the three Weird Sisters.
To you they have showed some truth.

Theme
Night torches and no stars emphasise darkness, linking with evil

Performance
Banquo could look towards heaven

Character
Banquo can't sleep and has bad thoughts showing his suspicions

Character
Although he says he is a friend the audience already know Macbeth can't be trusted.
We know he is lying in his pompous apology

Language
Words to do with weight emphasise how serious Banquo's suspicions are

Language
These words emphasise the King's happiness and generosity, and contrast with the evil about to take place

Theme
Dreams reveal the power of evil

Performance

Macbeth can gesture with his hands to show he doesn't think of the witches, but his voice could give the audience a different impression

Language

Does Macbeth use the royal 'we' by accident or in anticipation? 'Business' is Macbeth's usual euphemism for murder, which conceals its bloody reality

Character

Macbeth is tempting Banquo with promises of honours in the future

Character

Banquo is careful to say he won't do anything bad that might lose him his good reputation

Language

Words like 'fatal', 'gouts of blood' and 'bloody business' emphasise the sense of evil

MACBETH
I think not of them.
Yet when we can entreat an hour to serve,
We would spend it in some words upon that business,
If you would grant the time.

BANQUO
At your kind'st leisure.

MACBETH
If you shall cleave to my consent, when 'tis,
It shall make honour for you.

BANQUO
So I lose none
In seeking to augment it, but still keep
My bosom franchised, and allegiance clear,
I shall be counselled.

MACBETH
Good repose the while.

BANQUO
Thanks sir, the like to you!
                    [Exeunt BANQUO and FLEANCE

MACBETH
Go bid thy mistress, when my drink is ready,
She strike upon the bell. Get thee to bed.
                    [Exit SERVANT
Is this a dagger which I see before me,
The handle toward my hand? Come let me clutch thee.
I have thee not, and yet I see thee still.
Art thou not, fatal vision, sensible
To feeling as to sight? Or art thou but
A dagger of the mind, a false creation,
Proceeding from the heat-oppressed brain?
I see thee yet, in form as palpable
As this which now I draw.
Thou marshall'st me the way that I was going,
And such an instrument I was to use.
Mine eyes are made the fools o' th' other senses,
Or else worth all the rest. I see thee still;
And on thy blade and dudgeon gouts of blood,
Which was not so before. There's no such thing.
It is the bloody business which informs
Thus to mine eyes. Now o'er the one half-world

Character

Macbeth pretends to be unconcerned about the witches, showing how he is being taken over by his evil thoughts

Language

The polite language Macbeth and Banquo use shows they are wary of one another

Performance

Macbeth should look surprised and try to catch the dagger in his hands

Theme

A dagger of the mind shows the power of the evil

Character

Macbeth ignores the warning of the vision because he's in the grip of his evil ambition

Theme

Nature or normal life is asleep and witchcraft celebrates, emphasising the theme of evil

Character

Macbeth knows that if he keeps thinking about the evil of the murder he might change his mind

Nature seems dead, and wicked dreams abuse
The curtained sleep; witchcraft celebrates
Pale Hecate's offerings; and withered murder,
Alarumed by his sentinel the wolf,
Whose howl's his watch, thus with his stealthy pace,
With Tarquin's ravishing strides, towards his design
Moves like a ghost. Thou sure and firm-set earth,
Hear not my steps, which way they walk, for fear
Thy very stones prate of my whereabout,
And take the present horror from the time,
Which now suits with it. Whiles I threat,
he lives:
Words to the heat of deeds too cold breath gives.
                                        [*A bell rings*
I go, and it is done. The bell invites me.
Hear it not Duncan, for it is a knell
That summons thee to heaven or to hell. [*Exit*

Theme

Even the stones of the castle seem to be aware of the evil about to happen

Performance

The bell could make Macbeth jump before he goes out stealthily to emphasise the danger

Language

Knell, a bell indicating a death sums up all the references to death, fear and murder in the speech

ACT 2, SCENE 2
The same.
Enter LADY MACBETH

Language

'fatal bellman' links with 'knell' in Macbeth's speech, adding to sense of doom

Performance

Lady Macbeth should jump when she hears the owl's cry to emphasise tension

Performance

Sudden shout should make Lady Macbeth hold her hand to her mouth in anxiety

Character

'He could not miss 'em' shows that Lady Macbeth still doubts Macbeth's determination

LADY MACBETH
That which hath made them drunk hath made me bold;
What hath quench'd them hath given me fire.
Hark! Peace!
It was the owl that shrieked, the fatal bellman,
Which gives the stern'st good night. He is about it.
The doors are open; and the surfeited grooms
Do mock their charge with snores. I have drugged their possets,
That death and nature do contend about them,
Whether they live or die.

MACBETH
[*Within*] Who's there? What ho!

LADY MACBETH
Alack, I am afraid they have awaked,
And 'tis not done. Th' attempt and not the deed
Confounds us. Hark! I laid their daggers ready,
He could not miss 'em. Had he not resembled
My father as he slept, I had done't.

Character

'Bold' and 'fire' show how much she is excited by the murder

Language

'Drunk', 'quench'd', 'snores', 'drugged' add to the theme of sleep and death

Character

Lady Macbeth shows she isn't completely cold and hard when seeing the King reminds her of her father

Language
Unnatural animal sounds reinforce the theme of evil

Language
Sequence of short questions and answers emphasises fear and tension

Character
Lady Macbeth is still criticising her husband for his weakness

Theme
Disturbed sleep shows how things aren't well in the castle

Character
Macbeth is so horrified by what he has done that he can't help talking about the scene of the murder

Language
Religious words contrast with and emphasise the evil of the murder

Enter MACBETH
My husband!

MACBETH
I have done the deed. Didst thou not hear a noise?

LADY MACBETH
I heard the owl scream and the crickets cry.
Did not you speak?

MACBETH
When?

LADY MACBETH
Now.

MACBETH
As I descended?

LADY MACBETH
Ay.

MACBETH
Hark!
Who lies i' th' second chamber?

LADY MACBETH
Donalbain.

MACBETH
This is a sorry sight.
[*Looks on his hands*]

LADY MACBETH
A foolish thought, to say a sorry sight.

MACBETH
There's one did laugh in's sleep, and one cried
'Murder!'
That they did wake each other. I stood and heard them.
But they did say their prayers, and addressed them
Again to sleep.

LADY MACBETH
There are two lodged together.

MACBETH
One cried 'God bless us!' and 'Amen!' the other,
As they had seen me with these hangman's hands.
Listening their fear, I could not say 'Amen',
When they did say 'God bless us!'

LADY MACBETH
Consider it not so deeply.

Performance
As he enters, Macbeth should look horrified as he realises he has done the murder

Performance
Macbeth should move stealthily so no one can hear him

Performance
As they ask the questions and say the short lines, Macbeth and his wife should look around them fearfully

Performance
Macbeth should look at his hands showing sorrow and fear

This is a stage direction

Character
Lady Macbeth is not sympathetic to her husband's horror – she simply states the facts and tells him not to worry so much

Character

Macbeth shows how much he is worried and feels guilty when he asks why he couldn't pray

Character

Macbeth's long speech shows how worried he is about what he has done

Character

Lady Macbeth interrupts his speech, showing her impatience with him

Theme

The murder has stopped sleep so people can't be made well

Performance

Lady Macbeth could grab her husband and try to shake him out of his thoughts

Character

Macbeth has now lost his bravery and can't return to the scene of the murder

Performance

Lady Macbeth snatches the daggers from him and pushes him away

Theme

The possibility of madness is mentioned if they think too much about the murder

Language

Repetition of 'sleep no more' emphasises his mental torture and the theme of sleep

Character

Lady Macbeth shows how practical she is and her lack of concern about the murder

Theme

The similarities between sleep and death are emphasised

Character

Lady Macbeth is practical and thinks of ways to hide their guilt

---

MACBETH

But wherefore could not I pronounce 'Amen'?
I had most need of blessing, and 'Amen'
Stuck in my throat.

LADY MACBETH

These deeds must not be thought
After these ways; so, it will make us mad.

MACBETH

Methought I heard a voice cry 'Sleep no more!
Macbeth does murder sleep,' the innocent sleep,
Sleep that knits up the ravelled sleave of care,
The death of each day's life, sore labour's bath,
Balm of hurt minds, great nature's second course,
Chief nourisher in life's feast.

LADY MACBETH

What do you mean?

MACBETH

Still it cried 'Sleep no more!' to all the house.
Glamis hath murdered sleep, and therefore Cawdor
Shall sleep no more, Macbeth shall sleep no more.

LADY MACBETH

Who was it that thus cried? Why worthy
Thane,
You do unbend your noble strength, to think
So brainsickly of things. Go get some water,
And wash this filthy witness from your hand.
Why did you bring these daggers from the place?
They must lie there. Go carry them, and smear
The sleepy grooms with blood.

MACBETH

I'll go no more.
I am afraid to think what I have done.
Look on't again I dare not.

LADY MACBETII

Infirm of purpose!
Give me the daggers. The sleeping and the dead
Are but as pictures. 'Tis the eye of childhood
That fears a painted devil. If he do bleed,
I'll gild the faces of the grooms withal,
For it must seem their guilt.
                    [*Exit. Knock within*

MACBETH
Whence is that knocking?
How is't with me, when every noise appals me?
What hands are here? Ha! They pluck out mine eyes.
Will all great Neptune's ocean wash this blood
Clean from my hand? No, this my hand will rather
The multitudinous seas incarnadine,
Making the green one red.

Enter LADY MACBETH

LADY MACBETH
My hands are of your colour; but I shame
To wear a heart so white. [*Knock within*]
I hear a knocking
At the south entry. Retire we to our chamber.
A little water clears us of this deed.
How easy is it then! Your constancy
Hath left you unattended. [*Knock within*]
Hark, more knocking.
Get on your nightgown, lest occasion call us,
And show us to be watchers. Be not lost
So poorly in your thoughts.

MACBETH
To know my deed, 'twere best not know myself.
                              [*Knock within*
Wake Duncan with thy knocking. I would thou couldst.
                              [*Exeunt*

Performance
Macbeth should start and look surprised when the knocking is heard, and then look at his hands

Theme
The blood that can't be washed away shows how evil remains

Language
'White', 'unattended' and 'poorly' all show Macbeth as weak

Character
Macbeth is horrified at what he has done

Theme
Sleep and death are compared, showing how similar they can appear, but they are totally different

Language
The vision of the seas turning red emphasises the effect of the murder

Character
Lady Macbeth says she would be ashamed to be afraid like her husband

Theme
The theme of evil is continued by Lady Macbeth saying it can be washed away easily

Performance
Lady Macbeth could push her husband as she tries to get him to make sure they are not found out

Extract 2: Act 5, Scenes 3, 4 and 5

ACT 5, SCENE 3

Macbeth's castle
Enter MACBETH, DOCTOR, *and* ATTENDANTS

MACBETH
Bring me no more reports, <u>let them fly all</u>.
<u>Till Birnam wood remove to Dunsinane,</u>
<u>I cannot taint with fear</u>. What's the <u>boy</u> Malcolm?
Was he not born of woman? The spirits that know
All mortal consequences have pronounced me thus:
'Fear not Macbeth, <u>no man that's born of woman</u>
<u>Shall e'er have power upon thee</u>.' Then fly false thanes,
And mingle with the English <u>epicures</u>.
The mind I sway by, and the heart I bear,
Shall never sag with doubt, nor shake with fear.

Enter a SERVANT

The <u>devil damn thee</u> black, thou <u>cream</u>-faced loon.
Where gott'st thou that goose look?

SERVANT
There is ten thousand –

MACBETH
Geese, villain?

SERVANT
Soldiers sir.

MACBETH
Go prick thy face, and over-red thy fear,
Thou <u>lily</u>-livered boy. What soldiers, <u>patch</u>?
Death of thy soul, those <u>linen</u> cheeks of thine
Are counsellors to fear. What soldiers, <u>whey</u>-face?

SERVANT
The English force, so please you.

MACBETH
<u>Take thy face hence</u>.

[*Exit* SERVANT]

Theme
The danger of the supernatural is clear. The prophecies make Macbeth think he can't be harmed

Character
Macbeth repeats the fact that he doesn't feel fear and all the witches' reasons, showing he is trying to reassure himself

Character
Macbeth takes out his anger on his servant, showing that he is more anxious than he looks

Performance
Macbeth should be angry and push the servant or gesture at him to make him go

Performance
Macbeth should enter very angrily, waving his arms to emphasise his anger

Language
The word 'boy' makes Malcolm seem weak and 'epicures' makes the English seem polite and not warlike

Language
'Cream', 'lily', 'linen', 'whey' are all words suggesting paleness. They show Macbeth being rude to the servant, but they also emphasise the servant's fear of the huge English army

Character

Macbeth realises how much his life has declined and he is ready to die

Character

Macbeth thinks about all the good things he will not enjoy as an old man

Language

All the good words like 'love' and 'honour' are contrasted with 'curses' and 'mouth-honour', which is falseness

Theme

The evil continues to spread over the whole country, with Macbeth's soldiers terrorising and murdering people

Language

Images of weeding a garden, medicine and cleaning emphasise the need for the evil to be removed

Seyton! – I am sick at heart,
When I behold – Seyton, I say! – This push
Will cheer me ever, or disseat me now.
I have lived long enough. My way of life
Is fallen into the sear, the yellow leaf;
And that which should accompany old age,
As honour, love, obedience, troops of friends,
I must not look to have; but in their stead
Curses, not loud but deep, mouth-honour, breath
Which the poor heart would fain deny, and dare not.
Seyton!

Enter SEYTON

SEYTON
What's your gracious pleasure?

MACBETH
What news more?

SEYTON
All is confirmed my lord, which was reported.

MACBETH
I'll fight till from my bones my flesh be hacked.
Give me my armour.

SEYTON
'Tis not needed yet.

MACBETH
I'll put it on.
Send out more horses, skirr the country round,
Hang those that talk of fear. Give me mine armour.
How does your patient, doctor?

DOCTOR
Not so sick my lord,
As she is troubled with thick-coming fancies
That keep her from her rest.

MACBETH
Cure her of that.
Canst thou not minister to a mind diseased,
Pluck from the memory a rooted sorrow,
Raze out the written troubles of the brain,
And with some sweet oblivious antidote
Cleanse the stuffed bosom of that perilous stuff
Which weighs upon the heart?

DOCTOR
Therein the patient
Must minister to himself.

Theme

'Sick at heart' links with the theme of disease and evil

Language

'Sear' means withered and with 'yellow' suggests autumn leaves – Macbeth is ready to fall like a leaf

Performance

Macbeth could shudder as he shakes off his despair; he could then raise himself to his full height as he says he will fight

Theme

The disease affects the mind, showing the way the murder has consequences for the two killers

Character

Macbeth is talking about his own mind as well as his wife's

Character
Macbeth's anger shows that he knows the doctor is correct – only Macbeth can cure himself

Performance
Macbeth should show he has decided to act by rushing to put on his armour

Theme
Macbeth thinks the English army is another disease infecting his country but it is actually the cure

Performance
The doctor could look very clearly at the audience to show how keen he is to get away from the castle

Theme
The noise and colour of the army show the brightness of good contrasting with dark evil

MACBETH
Throw physic to the dogs, I'll none of it.
Come, put mine armour on; give me my staff.
Seyton, send out. Doctor, the thanes fly from me.
Come sir, dispatch. If thou couldst, doctor, cast
The water of my land, find her disease,
And purge it to a sound and pristine health,
I would applaud thee to the very echo,
That should applaud again. Pull't off, I say.
What rhubarb, senna, or what purgative drug,
Would scour these English hence? Hear'st thou of them?

DOCTOR
Ay my good lord; your royal preparation
Makes us hear something.

MACBETH
Bring it after me.
I will not be afraid of death and bane,
Till Birnam forest come to Dunsinane.
                [Exeunt all but DOCTOR

DOCTOR
Were I from Dunsinane away, and clear,
Profit again should hardly draw me here.

ACT 5, SCENE 4

Birnam wood.
Enter, with drum and colours, MALCOLM, SIWARD and
YOUNG SIWARD, MACDUFF, MENTEITH, CAITHNESS,
ANGUS, LENNOX, ROSS, *and* SOLDIERS, *marching*

MALCOLM
Cousins, I hope the days are near at hand
That chambers will be safe.

MENTEITH
We doubt it nothing.

SIWARD
What wood is this before us?

MENTEITH
The wood of Birnam.

Theme
The disease in the minds of the Macbeths is reflected in the country

Language
Words to do with treatment – 'purge', 'drug', 'scour' – emphasise theme of disease

Character
Macbeth repeats the witches' promise, showing he is trying to reassure himself that he can't die

Performance
The actors should look proud and confident and make plenty of noise to contrast with the fear in Macbeth's castle

Language
The word 'safe' makes an instant contrast with the evil in Macbeth's castle and 'chambers' reminds the audience of the murder

Character

Malcolm shows he is a leader by giving confident orders – not a 'boy' as Macbeth called him

Theme

Macbeth's soldiers are forced to follow him, showing bad leadership contrasting with Malcolm's good leadership

Language

'Famine' and 'ague' (disease) again show Macbeth's evil because he doesn't just want to beat the army but to kill them painfully

This is a stage direction

Performance

The cry should make everyone stop and look around them

MALCOLM
Let every soldier hew him down a bough,
And bear't before him, thereby shall we shadow
The numbers of our host, and make discovery
Err in report of us.

SOLDIERS
It shall be done.

SIWARD
We learn no other but the confident tyrant
Keeps still in Dunsinane, and will endure
Our setting down before 't.

MALCOLM
'Tis his main hope.
For where there is advantage to be gone,
Both more and less have given him the revolt,
And none serve with him but constrained things,
Whose hearts are absent too.

MACDUFF
Let our just censures
Attend the true event, and put we on
Industrious soldiership.

SIWARD
The time approaches
That will with due decision make us know
What we shall say we have and what we owe.
Thoughts speculative their unsure hopes relate,
But certain issue strokes must arbitrate;
Towards which advance the war.
                            [Exeunt, marching

ACT 5 SCENE 5

Dunsinane
Enter, with drum and colours, MACBETH, SEYTON, *and*
SOLDIERS

MACBETH
Hang out our banners on the outward walls.
The cry is still 'They come'. Our castle's strength
Will laugh a siege to scorn. Here let them lie
Till famine and the ague eat them up.
Were they not forced with those that should be ours,
We might have met them dareful, beard to beard,
And beat them backward home.
                        [A cry of women within
What is that noise?

SEYTON
It is the cry of women, my good lord.   [Exit

Theme

The size of the army is disguised linking to the theme of illusion and reality

Language

'Just', 'true' and 'certain' emphasise the way goodness and morality are being brought into the evil of Macbeth's rule by Malcolm's army

Character

Macbeth is still defiant because he believes he can't be beaten as the witches prophesised

Theme

Many of Macbeth's soldiers have joined Malcolm's army, showing how Macbeth is losing his power as a leader

MACBETH
I have almost forgot the taste of fears.
The time has been, my senses would have cooled
To hear a night-shriek, and my fell of hair
Would at a dismal treatise rouse and stir
As life were in't. I have supped full with horrors;
Direness, familiar to my slaughterous thoughts,
Cannot once start me.

Enter SEYTON

Wherefore was that cry?

SEYTON
The Queen, my lord, is dead.

MACBETH
She should have died hereafter;
There would have been a time for such a word.
Tomorrow, and tomorrow, and tomorrow,
Creeps in this petty pace from day to day,
To the last syllable of recorded time;
And all our yesterdays have lighted fools
The way to dusty death. Out, out, brief candle!
Life's but a walking shadow, a poor player,
That struts and frets his hour upon the stage,
And then is heard no more. It is a tale
Told by an idiot, full of sound and fury,
Signifying nothing.

Enter a MESSENGER

Thou comest to use thy tongue. Thy story quickly.

MESSENGER
Gracious my lord,
I should report that which I say I saw,
But know not how to do't.

MACBETH
Well, say, sir.

MESSENGER
As I did stand my watch upon the hill,
I looked toward Birnam, and anon methought,
The wood began to move.

MACBETH
Liar and slave!

MESSENGER
Let me endure your wrath, if't be not so.
Within this three mile may you see it coming.
I say, a moving grove.

MACBETH
If thou speak'st false,
Upon the next tree shalt thou hang alive
Till famine cling thee. If thy speech be sooth,
I care not if thou dost for me as much.
I pull in resolution, and begin
To doubt th'equivocation of the fiend,
That lies like truth: 'Fear not, till Birnam wood
Do come to Dunsinane'; and now a wood
Comes toward Dunsinane. Arm, arm, and out!
If this which he avouches does appear,
There is nor flying hence, nor tarrying here.
I 'gin to be aweary of the sun,
And wish th'estate o' th' world were now
undone.
Ring the alarum bell! Blow wind, come wrack,
At least we'll die with harness on our back.
                              [Exeunt]

Performance
The messenger should speak up and stand up to Macbeth

Language
'Lies', 'doubt', 'equivocation' emphasise Macbeth's realisation that the witches have tricked him with false promises

Performance
There should be loud noise and the actor playing Macbeth should shout loudly and could charge off the stage

Theme
Murder is threatened again

Character
Macbeth is no longer concerned whether or not he dies

Theme
A sense of hopelessness and despair is the final result of the murders

Character
Even though he has lost hope, Macbeth is still ready to fight bravely

Response graph for Macbeth and Lady Macbeth

Mark a point above or below the line to show whether your feelings about Macbeth are positive or negative at each episode described below. Then, using a different colour, plot your feelings about Lady Macbeth.

EPISODE	POSITIVE 10 9 8 7 6 5 4 3 2 1	NEGATIVE 1 2 3 4 5 6 7 8 9 10
Witches meet Macbeth and Banquo on the heath		
Witches' predictions begin to come true		
Duncan ennobles Macbeth		
Lady Macbeth hears of Duncan's visit to Glamis		
Lady Macbeth persuades Macbeth to murder Duncan		
Macbeth agonises over killing Duncan, who is a guest		
Banquo discovers Duncan's murder		
Banquo is murdered on Macbeth's orders		
Macbeth sees Banquo's ghost at the feast		
The witches show Macbeth visions, but their words deceive him		
Macbeth has Lady Macduff murdered		
Lady Macbeth is driven mad by her guilt		
Macbeth is alone and in despair but fights on to the last		
Macduff kills Macbeth and Duncan becomes King		

Macbeth's character PEE grid

Working with a partner, talk about the statements in the first column, then tick the appropriate box, give your evidence from the set scenes and explain your thinking.

Statement	Response	✔	✔	Evidence/Explanation
Macbeth is brave	Definitely		✔	He is brave in battle, because when he knows he is doomed, he says: 'At least we'll die with harness on our back' and goes out bravely.
	Yes, on balance			
	Not really			
	No way			
Macbeth is a weak character	Definitely			
	Yes, on balance			
	Not really			
	No way			
Macbeth's ambition is his downfall	Definitely			
	Yes, on balance			
	Not really			
	No way			
Macbeth is cruel	Definitely			
	Yes, on balance			
	Not really			
	No way			
Macbeth loves Lady Macbeth	Definitely			
	Yes, on balance			
	Not really			
	No way			
Macbeth is a victim who deserves our sympathy	Definitely			
	Yes, on balance			
	Not really			
	No way			
Macbeth is a villain who deserves what he gets	Definitely			
	Yes, on balance			
	Not really			
	No way			

Focuses

Using different coloured highlighters, match the points below with the quotations that provide the evidence for them.

Focus on character

Extract 1

Points	Quotations
Macbeth is tormented by what he is about to do – to kill his King, even though he is a guest.	… art thou but A dagger of the mind, a false creation, Proceeding from the heat-oppressed brain?
Macbeth fears that he is damned by what he has done.	It is the bloody business which informs Thus to mine eyes.
Macbeth has lost his peace of mind by murdering his King.	I had most need of blessing, and 'Amen' Stuck in my throat.
	I am afraid to think what I have done. Look on't again I dare not.
	To know my deed, 'twere best not know myself
	… Macbeth shall sleep no more.

Extract 2

Points	Quotations
Macbeth is brave, but partly because he believes that he cannot die.	The mind I sway by, and the heart I bear, Shall never sag with doubt, nor shake with fear.
Killing his King has not brought Macbeth the satisfaction he sought.	… The spirits that know All mortal consequences have pronounced me thus: 'Fear not Macbeth, no man that's born of woman Shall e'er have power upon thee'.
Macbeth's relationship with his wife has changed – they have not been partners for some time.	… that which should accompany old age, As honour, love, obedience, troops of friends, I must not look to have
Macbeth realises that the weird sisters have deceived him.	She should have died hereafter; There would have been a time for such a word.
	Life's but a walking shadow, a poor player, That struts and frets his hour upon the stage, And then is heard no more. It is a tale Told by an idiot, full of sound and fury, Signifying nothing.
	I pull in resolution, and begin To doubt th'equivocation of the fiend, That lies like truth
	Blow wind, come wrack, At least we'll die with harness on our back.

Focus on themes

Look at the points below about themes. By using different coloured highlighters try to match them with the quotations that give the evidence for the points and then think what the impact the words you quote would have on an audience.

Points	Quotations

Good/evil
 	
• Macbeth becomes evil, deceitful and disloyal. Lies come easily to him now and the truth does not matter since darkness, linked with evil, covers his crimes.
• Macbeth fears damnation and dare not look on dead Duncan.
• Evil (i.e. Macbeth) is a 'disease' in the body of Scotland.
• Malcolm, supported by the English, represents goodness, and the 'cure' for that disease, but good has to be disguised in Macbeth's Scotland.
• Good does eventually triumph: at the end of Act 5, Scene 5 Macbeth goes out to be killed by the man whose family he has murdered.
	Extract 1
	• … witchcraft celebrates
	  Pale Hecate's offerings
	• Now o'er the one half-world
	  Nature seems dead, and wicked dreams abuse
	  The curtained sleep
	• Macbeth lies about the weird sisters – 'I think not of them'
	• I am afraid to think what I have done.
	  Look on't again I dare not.
	
	Extract 2
	• … The spirits that know
	  All mortal consequences
	• … the fiend,
	  That lies like truth
	• … If thou couldst, doctor, cast
	  The water of my land, find her disease,
	  And purge it
	• … I have supped full with horrors;

Guilt and despair
 	
• Macbeth has said 'I go and it is done', but his guilt shows immediately.
• Lady Macbeth is not ambitious for herself, but for Macbeth. She is not at all remorseful at first, but eventually her guilt drives her mad.
• Macbeth kills Duncan because he is ambitious, but knows he has done wrong.
• Murdering Duncan does not bring Macbeth inner peace or guarantee his safety in the outer world.
	Extract 1
	• I had most need of blessing, and 'Amen'
	  Stuck in my throat.
	• Macbeth does murder sleep
	• To know my deed, 'twere best not know myself
	• Will all great Neptune's ocean wash this blood
	  Clean from my hand?
	• I am afraid to think what I have done.
	  Look on't again I dare not.
	• How is't with me, when every noise appals me?
	  LADY MACBETH
	• A little water clears us of this deed.
	  How easy is it then!
	• Wake Duncan with thy knocking. I would thou couldst.
	
	Extract 2
	• … She is troubled with thick-coming fancies
	  That keep her from her rest.
	  MACBETH
	• Canst thou not minister to a mind diseased
	• I have lived long enough. My way of life
	  Is fallen into the sear, the yellow leaf;
	• And that which should accompany old age,
	  As honour, love, obedience, troops of friends,
	  I must not look to have
	• Life's but a walking shadow, a poor player,
	  That struts and frets his hour upon the stage,
	  And then is heard no more.
	• I 'gin to be aweary o'th sun,
	  And wish th' estate o' th' world were now undone.

Illusion and reality
 	
• Hard to tell what is real and what is not. e.g Is the dagger real or unreal? The impossible is seen at the end – a moving grove.
• Ambition was only an illusion – the reality for Macbeth is despair. He feels like an actor whose role is an illusion.
• Lady Macbeth seems tough and unnatural, but proves vulnerable and human.
	Extract 1
	• It is the bloody business which informs
	  Thus to mine eyes.
	• I am afraid to think what I have done;
	  Look on't again I dare not.
	• What hands are here? Ha! They pluck out mine eyes.
	  LADY MACBETH
	• … The sleeping and the dead
	  Are but as pictures.
	• A little water clears us of this deed.
	  Get on your nightgown, lest occasion call us, And show us to be watchers.
	
	Extract 2
	• I have lived long enough. My way of life
	  Is fallen into the sear, the yellow leaf …
	• Life's but a walking shadow, a poor player,
	  That struts and frets his hour upon the stage,
	  And then is heard no more.
	  MACBETH
	• … begin
	  To doubt th' equivocation of the fiend,
	  That lies like truth

Focus on language

Look at the points below about language. By using different coloured highlighters try to match them with the quotations that give the evidence for the points and then think what impact the words you quote would have on an audience.

Points	Quotations
Language 1	**Extract 1**
• The images in Macbeth's speeches show us – that he knows his intentions are evil.	• *Nature seems dead, and wicked dreams abuse* *The curtained sleep; witchcraft celebrates*
• This is a play about deception; the images of sight that Macbeth refers to constantly show us that he does not know whether to trust what he sees:	• *Pale Hecate's offerings; and withered murder,* *... towards his design* *Moves like a ghost.*
○ see before me	• *... Or art thou but* *A dagger of the mind, a false creation,* *Proceeding from the heat-oppressed brain?*
○ fatal vision	• *Mine eyes are made the fools o' th' other senses,* *Or else worth all the rest.*
○ informs thus to mine eyes.	• *Will all great Neptune's ocean wash this blood* *Clean from my hand? No, this my hand will rather* *The multitudinous seas incarnadine,* *Making the green one red.*
• His belief in what the witches show him proves to be his downfall when a wood seems to start moving.	• *Methought I heard a voice cry 'Sleep no more!* *Macbeth does murder sleep'*
• Macbeth was never a true king – he merely acted the part.	
• Images of sound are increasingly powerful in these murder scenes – from the bell that summons Duncan to heaven or hell to the knocking at the south entry.	
	Extract 2
	• *... begin* *To doubt th' equivocation of the fiend,* *That lies like truth.*
	• *... If thou couldst, doctor, cast* *The water of my land, find her disease,* *And purge it to a sound and pristine health*
	• *... My way of life* *Is fallen into the sear, the yellow leaf*
	• *... Out, out, brief candle!* *Life's but a walking shadow, a poor player,* *That struts and frets his hour upon the stage,* *And then is heard no more.*
Language 2	**Extract 1**
• Images of colour run through the scene after the murder, and in the later scenes.	• *My hands are of your colour; but I shame* *To wear a heart so white.*
• The tension when Macbeth re-enters after killing Duncan is reflected in the sharp, staccato dialogue.	• *How is't with me, when every noise appals me?*
• In the later extract Macbeth is largely talking to himself or to servants – no-one is left to listen as an equal.	LADY MACBETH *Did not you speak?*
• Near the end, Macbeth has only a bitter taste of despair in his mouth.	MACBETH *When?*
	LADY MACBETH *Now.*
	MACBETH *As I descended?*
	LADY MACBETH *Ay.*
	MACBETH *Hark!*
	Extract 2
	• *... damn thee black, thou cream-faced loon.*
	• *Go prick thy face, and over-red thy fear,* *Thou lily-livered boy.*
	• *... linen cheeks*
	• *... the yellow leaf*
	• *And then is heard no more. It is a tale* *Told by an idiot, full of sound and fury,* *Signifying nothing.*
	• *I have almost forgot the <u>taste of fears</u>.* *... I have <u>supped</u> full with horrors*
	• *... What's the boy Malcolm?* *Was he not born of woman?*

> Words about eating make us think of life as a meal which has made us sick

Focus on performance

Look at the points below about performance. By using different coloured highlighters, try to match the points with evidence in the form of quotations.

Extract 1

Points	Quotations
• Might a director want a darkened, menacing stage?	… There's husbandry in heaven, Their candles are all out.
• The tension between Macbeth and Banquo needs to be in words as well as their movement on stage – they are no longer close comrades.	Being unprepared, Our will became the servant to defect …
• Macbeth's apology as a host sounds false. He should look as if he is hiding something, as when he lies about thinking of the witches.	I think not of them. If you shall cleave to my consent, when 'tis, It shall make honour for you.
• Macbeth hints at the benefit to Banquo of cooperating with him – Banquo's reaction could be a distancing of himself from Macbeth.	BANQUO wants to … keep My bosom franchised, and allegiance clear
• Making credible Macbeth's a vision of a dagger is quite a challenge to any actor and director: should it be visible to the audience or not?	Is this a dagger which I see before me, The handle toward my hand?
• Macbeth embraces the powers of darkness and evil as he goes to murder Duncan.	Nature seems dead … witchcraft celebrates … the present horror
• Lady Macbeth's anticipation of discovery heightens the tension – she is relieved that it is Macbeth who appears.	My husband!
• The staccato conversation crackles with more tension.	LADY MACBETH Did not you speak? MACBETH When? LADY MACBETH Now. MACBETH As I descended? LADY MACBETH Ay.
• The realisation that Macbeth has carried out the daggers needs to be convincing to the audience (e.g. by keeping them hidden from Lady Macbeth) as does Macbeth's refusal to revisit the scene of his crime.	MACBETH Hark! Why did you bring these daggers from the place? I am afraid to think what I have done. Look on't again I dare not.
• The knocking must come as a shock to the audience as well as to Macbeth. He and Lady Macbeth stumble away, with Lady Macbeth in control of herself and her husband.	Whence is that knocking?

Extract 2

Points	Quotations
• Macbeth is now alone except for servants, but still believes in the protection of the prophecies. His treatment of his remaining servants needs to have a manic fury about it, for example: pulling the armour on and off, shouting, storming round the stage. The servants should be visibly terrified.	I cannot taint with fear. Go prick thy face, and over-red thy fear, Thou lily-livered boy.
• When Macbeth talks of his wife's illness, we apply some of it to himself.	Canst thou not minister to a mind diseased, Pluck from the memory a rooted sorrow …
• Siward's language later in Scene 4 is rather pompous, but the soldiers' action of disguising themselves with tree branches should be done purposefully so that we realise this is a force to be reckoned with, led by someone fit to be king.	MALCOLM Let every soldier hew him down a bough, And bear't before him, thereby shall we shadow The numbers of our host …
• Macbeth is fierce until the cry of women breaks his mood. Conveying his mixture of emotions on hearing of his wife's death whilst preparing for battle is a real challenge to an actor.	I have almost forgot the taste of fears. She should have died hereafter; There would have been a time for such a word.
• When Macbeth reflects on his despair, it is important to give spoken emphasis to the images of a flickering candle, a poor player. (Lady Macbeth had a candle by her constantly.)	… Out, out, brief candle! Life's but a walking shadow, a poor player, That struts and frets his hour upon the stage, And then is heard no more.
• Macbeth's body language should show that he realises he has been deceived by the witches, but nevertheless he leaves with defiant bravery.	I pull in resolution, and begin To doubt th' equivocation of the fiend, That lies like truth … Blow wind, come wrack, At least we'll die with harness on our back.

The Key Stage 3 Shakespeare test

How to approach the test

Remember that:

- Your understanding of Shakespeare and the way he uses language is what is assessed – you will not be judged on how well you write, although the way you write does matter because it enables you to make your points effectively.
- 18 marks out of the 50 marks for reading are allocated to the Shakespeare test. No marks are given (or taken off) for spelling or expression.
- The extracts you will have to write about will be printed in the test paper. Don't make the mistake of writing about all the set scenes – concentrate on those two extracts.

And, by the way …

Since you will have to write about both extracts, you are not likely to be asked to focus on characters like Banquo or the Doctor who appear in only one of the extracts.

Revision

You can use this book to help with your preparation for the test by:

- Looking back at the illustrated outline of the play on pages 4 and 5 to remind yourself of the sequence of events.
- Making sure that you are familiar with the quotations about Macbeth and that you are used to telling other people what your thoughts about him are.
- Getting your head around the four 'big ideas' of character, language, themes and performance by talking with others about the points and quotations on pages 20–23.
- Making sure that any answer includes comment on the effect of language on an audience.
- Planning answers to some or all of the sample questions on page 26.
- Working out what are the strengths (and there are many) of the sample answer, and what could be done to improve it.
- Looking at the marking criteria on page 25 enough to understand why marks are awarded by the examiners, and making sure that you can do what is needed.

Top 10 tips for the test

1. Make sure you are familiar with the layout and style of questions by looking at tests from previous years.
2. Read the question aloud in your head two or three times until you realise what it is really asking you to do.
3. Keep in mind performances of the play that you have seen in the theatre or on video and remember what it was like acting out the set scenes with other people.
4. It is better to explore a few points in depth and discuss the effect of language in detail, than to offer a series of general comments.
5. Don't ever just tell the story – answer the question.
6. Time spent on planning is time well spent. Practise doing a plan in five minutes so that in the real test you can create a plan within ten minutes.
7. Plan so that your main points are in a sensible order that responds to the question.
8. Provide evidence in quotation or refer to what happens and what is said to support your points. (*Remember not to waste time copying out long quotations but do make sure you comment on the effect of language.*)
9. Make sure that your conclusion relates back to the question.
10. Leave time (but not too much!) at the end of the test to read through what you have written.

What do I need to remember about how the Shakespeare paper will be marked?
Your understanding of *Macbeth* is assessed only for reading:
* You are not expected to write about the play as a whole, but to refer to the extracts given on the test paper. These extracts will be taken from the set scenes which are on pages 6 to 17 of this booklet.

What will the question be on?
The question on *Macbeth* should be on <u>one</u> of the areas (or 'big ideas') below, although you can refer to the other areas, especially to language, as part of your answer:
* why characters behave as they do in the extracts given
* the impact of the language used in the extracts
* ideas, themes and issues that are relevant to the extracts
* how these extracts might be performed in the theatre.

How will my answer be marked?
The emphasis in marking will depend on the focus of the question, but generally answers are awarded level 5 or above if they:
* include comment on both of the extracts given on the paper
* reveal some understanding of character and dramatic action
* refer to the main features of the language in the extracts and the effect this language might have
* show some awareness of how an audience might respond
* illustrate points made by picking out words or phrases from the text as evidence.

What are the different mark bands about?
Working with a partner, look at the table below. It gives you the examiner's reasons for putting answers to a question about language in different mark bands. They have been jumbled up, so try to agree how to order them from 1 (lowest) to 6 (highest). Remember that the marking criteria always depend on the particular question asked.

Marking criteria (simplified version)	
The answer is mainly re-telling the story. There are a few comments about the ways characters behave, but not much explanation. The answer doesn't really answer the question that was asked.	
The answer shows understanding of the extracts and does mention the question. There is some comment on the attitudes and behaviour of characters and understanding of how these are presented through language and performance. Appropriate quotations support the points made in the answer.	
The answer really does tackle the question and shows understanding of the extracts. There is comment on features of language, and its impact on an audience, as well as on the attitudes and behaviour of characters. Well-chosen quotations support the points made in the answer.	
The answer shows a vague understanding of the question. Ideas are a bit sketchy and undeveloped, but there is some comment on the attitudes and behaviour of characters. The writer seems to have some understanding of how use of language helps to present characters and ideas. Quotations are linked with points.	
The answer is clearly focused on the question and shows thoughtful understanding. It shows insight into the attitudes and behaviour of characters. The answer analyses features of language and explores how language contributes to the presentation of character and ideas. The points made are relevant and are justified through carefully selected references to the text.	
This answer is not just an account, although it is more about what happens than about the language used. The explanation of characters' attitudes and behaviour shows understanding. It may include a few words or phrases from the extracts.	

Sample questions

The questions below are typical of the questions that could be set on Macbeth. You are not likely to be asked exactly the same question as any of these below, because these sample questions cover all of the set scenes, and in the test you will be given shorter extracts from the scenes. You always need to refer to both extracts in your answer.

Character

1. Do you think of Macbeth more as a victim or a villain?
2. How are the changes in the relationship between Macbeth and Lady Macbeth presented in these extracts?

Language

1. What differences do you notice in the language Macbeth uses when talking to others and when he is talking to himself?
2. How do Macbeth's words in these two extracts reveal changes in his thoughts and feelings?

Themes

1. What do these two extracts show about natural and unnatural behaviour?
2. How do these two extracts show the negative effects of ambition?

Performance

1. What advice would you give to an actor playing Macbeth on how to show the ways Macbeth has changed between these two extracts?
2. If you were directing a school performance of this play, how would you try to show the differences in Macbeth's behaviour between the two extracts?

Unpacking the question: an example

The need to refer to the two extracts

Show signals the need to write about what is said and what happens on stage.

What do these two extracts show about natural and unnatural behaviour?

Important to explain with evidence what is meant by natural and unnatural in the play, since this is a play about ideas as well as actions.

The behaviour of characters, especially but not only Macbeth, is the basis of the answer.

Sample answer

Is Macbeth a victim or a villain?

How I feel about Macbeth changes between the first extract and the second extract as a mixture of villain and victim but in the second extract he just seems like a villain.

In the first extract he begins by seeming a complete villain because he is planning the murder of the King. When he says 'While I threat he lives' it shows he is annoyed with himself for talking instead of getting on with the murder. Another point which shows he is a villain is when he tries to tempt Banquo to be evil as well because he offers Banquo some rewards when he says 'It shall make honour for you' but Banquo refuses.

Later in the first extract after he has murdered Duncan he seems more like a victim. When he looks at the blood on his hands and says 'this is a sorry sight' it is almost like he can't believe he has actually done it. He is upset that he can't pray 'I could not say Amen' which shows he wishes he hadn't murdered the King and it makes me feel he was tricked by the witches. What really makes him seem like a victim in the first extract is when Lady Macbeth is so horrible to him like when she says 'I shame to wear a heart so white' which shows she is ashamed of his weakness. This seems unfair because he did the murder and she didn't. At the end of the first extract he seems almost lost in his thoughts of his evil act and when he says ''twere best not know myself' he seems like a victim of the witches and Lady Macbeth.

In the second extract he seems very different because he has had more people murdered so he doesn't feel so guilty. In the first extract he seemed frightened but in the second he doesn't seem to be frightened of anything which is shown when he says 'I'll fight til from my bones my flesh be hack'd' so he doesn't care if he or any others die which is very evil. In the first extract he seemed like a victim of Lady Macbeth's bullying but in the second extract she is sick and he doesn't need her to tell him what to do.

Macbeth also shows he is a villain by the way he treats his messengers and servants when he calls them lots of names like 'cream faced loon' and 'lily-livered'. This shows he is a bully now because the servants can't answer back. When he hears that Lady Macbeth has died Macbeth shows how uncaring he is now because all he says is 'she should have died hereafter' and he doesn't seem at all upset. Malcolm emphasises how evil Macbeth has become when he tells the other leaders that Macbeth's soldiers are 'constrained' meaning forced to stay and their 'hearts are absent' which means they don't really want to fight for him any more as he is so bad.

In the second extract Macbeth is a totally evil villain but I still think he is also partly a victim because the witches tricked him and that has poisoned his mind. He says 'I have supp'd full with horrors' which shows how the witches' words have affected his mind.

(559 words)

Planning your answer

Spend at least 5 minutes on planning in the test. The time available for planning is limited, so use it well.

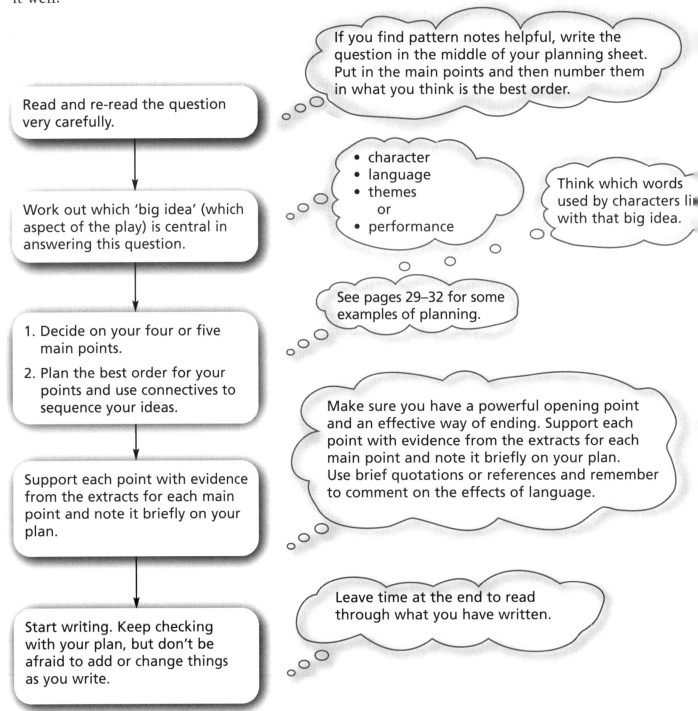

Read and re-read the question very carefully.

Work out which 'big idea' (which aspect of the play) is central in answering this question.

1. Decide on your four or five main points.

2. Plan the best order for your points and use connectives to sequence your ideas.

Support each point with evidence from the extracts for each main point and note it briefly on your plan.

Start writing. Keep checking with your plan, but don't be afraid to add or change things as you write.

If you find pattern notes helpful, write the question in the middle of your planning sheet. Put in the main points and then number them in what you think is the best order.

• character
• language
• themes
*   or*
• performance

Think which words used by characters li[nk] with that big idea.

See pages 29–32 for some examples of planning.

Make sure you have a powerful opening point and an effective way of ending. Support each point with evidence from the extracts for each main point and note it briefly on your plan. Use brief quotations or references and remember to comment on the effects of language.

Leave time at the end to read through what you have written.

Remember: marking 300 similar answers does get boring, so examiners appreciate a personal voice in an answer that does not just state the obvious.

Planning a character answer: number the four main points (in bold) in the order that you would put them in an answer.

My husband! is how Lady Macbeth thinks of Macbeth in the first extract.

Macbeth recognises that his wife's madness has been caused by guilt: *Can'st thou not minister to a mind diseased.* He seeks a *sweet oblivious antidote* for them both.

Macbeth and Lady Macbeth are so close at first that she can insult (*Infirm of purpose*) or command him (*Go get the daggers*).

Explain why certain words and images show changes in their relationship and have the effect on the audience that they do.

Lady Macbeth is the one in control after the murder – *My hands are of your colour, but I shame To wear a heart so white*

Give examples of actions that show how the relationship changes; that is, illustrate by evidence from the sections of text, picking out words or phrases and commenting on their effect.

She should have died hereafter comes as a shock – Macbeth does not have time to grieve for his wife's death.

Introduction: The changes are presented through words and actions on stage.

Macbeth and Lady Macbeth have lost contact by the 2nd extract: The two are not shown together on stage.

Lady Macbeth denies her own humanity for Macbeth. When they drift apart she cannot cope with her guilt when she is not in contact with Macbeth.

How are the changes in the relationship between Macbeth and Lady Macbeth presented in these extracts?

What do we learn about in *both* sections? That is, comment with understanding on character and behaviour.

Show awareness of audience response; that is, identify and comment on the impact of the text on the audience.

We see the intensity and closeness of their relationship at the time of the murder become so distant that Macbeth and Lady Macbeth do not appear together on stage in Act 5.

Having seen how much Lady Macbeth risks for Macbeth in Act 1, we react against him when his response to news of the death of his 'dearest love' is so brief that it seems uncaring.

In the first extract the two are together on stage, physically and psychologically in tune. By Act 5, each is alone and they do not meet. Macbeth hears of Lady Macbeth only via others such as the Doctor.

Planning a theme answer: number the four main points (in bold) in the order that you would put them in an answer.

the sere, the yellow leaf and I 'gin to be aweary o' the sun reveal that kingship has not brought Macbeth contentment.

Macbeth immediately regrets murdering his King – *To know my deed, 'twere best not know myself.*

The '*body*' of Scotland becomes '*diseased*', and since Macbeth is the cause because of his ambition, the cure is to kill him.

Tomorrow and tomorrow and tomorrow ... and the images of candle and poor player show us Macbeth's despair, despite achieving his ambition to become king.

Loyalty has been betrayed by Macbeth and since then *Both more and less have given him the revolt.* Scotland is in turmoil.

Explain why certain words and images have the effect on the audience that they do.

Give examples of actions that show the result of Macbeth's ambition; illustrating by evidence from the sections of text, picking out words or phrases.

Because Macbeth *could not say 'Amen'*, he feels that he is damned.

How do these two extracts show the negative effects of ambition?

Malcolm is king by right, not ambition, and we feel he represents the return of goodness and order.

Macbeth's own peace of mind (and Lady Macbeth's) are destroyed, along with the country's peace. Both inner and outer worlds suffer because of Macbeth's ambition.

Introduction: The negative effects of ambition are shown through characters' words and actions on stage

What do we learn from *both* **sections about the theme of ambition?**

Show awareness of audience response by identifying and commenting on the impact on the audience.

Disorder replaces order in the first extracts. The evil released across Scotland because of Macbeth's ambition has to be '*cured*' by the English invasion and Macbeth's death.

Kingship turns to despair for Macbeth – outer success does not bring him inner satisfaction just '*dusty death*'.

We realise that Macbeth's ambition made it easy for the weird sisters to trick him into becoming evil and that evil spread because of him. This costs him our sympathy.

Planning a language answer: number the four main points (in bold) in the order that you would put them in an answer.

Amen, God bless us, heaven and hell show that Macbeth fears damnation.

Macbeth's feelings change when he realises the witches have tricked him.
I pull in resolution, and begin To doubt th'equivocation of the fiend, That lies like truth.

Explain which words and images show us Macbeth's thoughts and feelings in the first extract and comment on the effect this language has.

As soon as he has killed Duncan, he is in fear: *I am afraid to think what I have done.*
Look on't again I dare not.

Give examples that show changes in how he is thinking and feeling and illustrate with evidence by picking out words or phrases, explaining the effect they have.

He hides the horror of murdering Duncan as a '*business*' and hopes *I go and it is done.*

Macbeth now regrets that his unnatural behaviour has deprived him of *that which should accompany old age, As honour, love, obedience , troops of friends, I must not look to have.*

How do Macbeth's words in these two extracts reveal changes in his thoughts and feelings?

The *Tomorrow* speech shows Macbeth as King, but in despair. His Queen is dead and life is a shadow, a poor player or *a tale Told by an idiot, full of sound and fury, Signifying nothing.*

Explain which words and images show us Macbeth's thoughts and feelings in the second extract.

Comment on the impact of Macbeth's words on the audience.

In extract 2, although he is King, life holds no more for Macbeth than the sense of loneliness, despair and *dusty death.* Betrayed by the witches, bravery is all he has left.

Macbeth's words and imagery enable us to share his fears (*Macbeth does murder Sleep*) and his final despair: *Tomorrow and tomorrow and tomorrow* ...His ambition has died before he dies

Macbeth's words let us see the suffering inside his mind – we know he has been evil, but we still care about him at the end, when he is still a bold fighter – *Blow wind, come wrack, At least we'll die with harness on our back.*

Planning a performance answer: number the four main points (in bold) in the order that you would put them in an answer.

Macbeth is torn between ambition and his sense that murdering his King is evil and will bring damnation. I would have his movements jerky as he says *Is this a dagger which I see before me ...* because he cannot grasp what is real and what is unreal.

Macbeth fears he has damned himself and would try (unsuccessfully) to pray when he says *Wherefore could I not pronounce 'Amen'?*

Putting his armour on, and taking it off again, reflects the swings of Macbeth's mind and mood.

Explain how your direction would bring out the impact of certain words and images in the first extract.

The longest pause in the play would be just before Macbeth says, *She should have died hereafter...* since he does not know how to voice his feelings.

Explain how your direction would bring out the impact of certain words and images in the second extract.

Macbeth would already be furtive in his approach to Banquo – sidling up to him and whispering rather than speaking loudly.

If you were directing this play for a school performance, how would you try to show the differences in Macbeth's behaviour between the two extracts?

Macbeth would shrink physically when he realises the witches have fooled him and he starts to **pull in resolution** the way he might pull a horse.

Give examples of how Macbeth's actions would show what he is feeling.

Comment on the impact of the performance on the audience.

Macbeth's distracted behaviour after the murder shows that he is no longer a soldier – he dare not return the daggers or look again on Duncan's body.

When Macbeth hears of the *moving grove* he would try to throttle the messenger, because he knows the witches have betrayed him and his tone is that of a tyrant.

I would hope that the audience would never totally hate Macbeth and that when he rushes out at the end, they would expect his death, but regret the loss of a brave man, whose crimes brought him no peace and cost him his soul.